Career Expert Files

What Social Workers Need to Know

Diane Lindsey Reeves

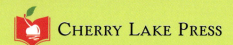

Published in the United States of America by Cherry Lake Publishing Group
Ann Arbor, Michigan
www.cherrylakepublishing.com

Reading Adviser: Beth Walker Gambro, MS, Ed., Reading Consultant, Yorkville, IL

Photo Credits: © Ground Picture/Shutterstock, cover; © SeventyFour/Shutterstock, 5, 7; © Media_Photos/Shutterstock, 7; © Africa Studio/Shutterstock, 8; © Chay_Tee/Shutterstock, 9; © Media_Photos/ Shutterstock, 11; © Pressmaster/Shutterstock, 12; © Edgar BJ/Shutterstock, 13; © DC Studio/Shutterstock, 14; © ViDI Studio/Shutterstock, 15; © fizkes/Shutterstock, 17; © Moffett, Public domain, via Wikimedia Commons, 18; © AnnaStills/Shutterstock, 19; © PeopleImages.com - Yuri A/Shutterstock, 21; © LightField Studios/Shutterstock, 22; © Mega Pixel/Shutterstock, 23; © Krakenimages.com/Shutterstock, 24; © nampix/Shutterstock, 25; © Drazen Zigic/Shutterstock, 27; © Pressmaster/Shutterstock, 28; © SynthEx/Shutterstock, 29; © Dragon Images/Shutterstock, 31

Copyright © 2026 by Cherry Lake Publishing Group
All rights reserved. No part of this book may be reproduced or utilized in any form or by any means without written permission from the publisher.

Cherry Lake Press is an imprint of Cherry Lake Publishing Group.

Library of Congress Cataloging-in-Publication Data has been filed and is available at catalog.loc.gov.

Cherry Lake Publishing Group would like to acknowledge the work of the Partnership for 21st Century Learning, a Network of Battelle for Kids. Please visit Battelle for Kids online for more information.

Printed in the United States of America

Note from publisher: Websites change regularly, and their future contents are outside of our control. Supervise children when conducting any recommended online searches for extended learning opportunities.

Diane Lindsey Reeves likes to write books that help students figure out what they want to be when they grow up. She mostly lives in Washington, D.C., but spends as much time as she can in North Carolina and South Carolina with her grandkids.

CONTENTS

Introduction:
In the Know | 4

Chapter 1:
Social Workers Know...That Life Gets Tough Sometimes | 6

Chapter 2:
Social Workers Know...All About Helping People | 10

Chapter 3:
Social Workers Know... The Tools of the Trade | 16

Chapter 4:
Social Workers Know...How to Work Safely | 20

Chapter 5:
Social Workers Know...How to Find the Job They Want | 26

Stop, Think, and Write | 30
Things to Do If You Want to Be a Social Worker | 30
Learn More | 31
Glossary, Index | 32

In the Know

Every career you can imagine has one thing in common: It takes an expert. Career experts need to know more about how to do a specific job than other people do. That's how everyone from plumber to rocket scientist gets their job done.

Sometimes it takes years of college study to learn what they need to know. Other times, people learn by working alongside someone who is already a career expert. No matter how they learn, it takes a career expert to do any job well.

Take social workers, for instance. Like other **first responders**, social workers help people. They work in the places people turn to when they have big problems. These include schools, hospitals, mental health clinics, and more.

The one thing that all social workers have in common is that they care. They want to help people. They do what they can to help people live better lives.

Social workers are good at:

- Showing compassion and empathy
- Helping people solve problems
- Staying calm in a crisis
- Providing emotional support and practical advice

CHAPTER 1

Social Workers Know... That Life Gets Tough Sometimes

Everyone has problems. Some problems people can figure out by themselves. Some problems get so big that people need help. Social workers step in here to offer a helping hand.

Maybe a family is struggling to pay their bills. They can't afford rent or food. Social workers can direct them to resources for help. This might mean connecting them with a homeless shelter or food bank. It could involve helping the adults in the family find jobs. They do what they can to help the family members get back on their feet.

In other cases, social workers help **immigrants** who come to the United States from other places. It is difficult to start a new life in a new country. Everything is unfamiliar.

Social workers work with all kinds of people, including adults and children. Anyone can ask for help from a social worker.

School social workers work in elementary, middle, and high schools. They help kids of all ages.

Sometimes immigrants do not speak English. Social workers help immigrants tap into resources that can help them communicate, find housing, and find jobs.

Some social workers work in schools. They help with problems that keep children from learning. They help students deal with personal or family issues. Sometimes they speak out when a child needs protection from abuse or neglect.

There are so many ways that social workers help. That's why they tend to specialize in certain kinds of problems. The problem could be drug dependence. It could be homelessness or hunger. Social workers make the world a better place one person at a time.

People decide to become social workers for different reasons. Some simply want to make life better for other people. Some want to fight for social justice and stick up for people who need protection. It's a career that matters and makes a difference. Is it a career you'd like to consider?

COMPASSION OR EMPATHY?

Compassion and empathy help us understand what other people are going through. Empathy usually comes first. It is when you understand another person's feelings. In a way, you may even feel their pain. Compassion is what sparks action. You see a problem and want to do something about it. Social workers use both empathy and compassion in their work.

CHAPTER 2

Social Workers Know… All About Helping People

The thing social workers need to know the most about is people. They study hard to better understand how humans behave. They learn what people need to thrive at different stages of life. They know that difficult circumstances can throw a person off track. They also know that the right kind of support can help people lead healthy, productive lives.

Many of the problems social workers deal with are very personal. It's important that they guard each client's privacy. The only time they can share a client's private information is if a client is at risk of hurting themselves or others. Situations that involve child or elder abuse must be reported to the proper authorities.

Social workers build trust with their clients. This helps clients to be honest with them.

Government housing can be hard to navigate. Social workers help make this process easier for those in need.

State governments have social service programs in place. They offer programs that provide family assistance and mental health services. Social workers must understand how these programs work. They must be familiar with programs that offer health care, housing, and legal support.

The first thing a social worker does when they meet a new client is **assess** the problem. They find out what help is needed and figure out the best way to provide it. In social worker terms, this means they assess the client's problems. Then they figure out how to **intervene** with solutions.

Health care is a big concern for parents. Social workers help make sure that all kids, regardless of outside circumstances, have the care they need.

Food banks are a crucial public resource. Most cities have them in order to help those who need food.

In certain situations, social workers give a voice to people who cannot speak up for themselves. They look for ways to change programs and laws to make them more useful. This is called **advocacy**. It is a way that social workers promote social justice. They can also be agents for changing systems to better serve people in need.

Three words that begin with the letter *C* explain skills every social worker needs to do their job. They need strong communication skills. This helps them connect with clients. They need the ability to **collaborate** with other people who can help. This includes networking with community resources like shelters and food banks. Social workers also need crisis management skills. They must stay calm and be ready to support clients during emergencies.

HELP THE HELPERS

Social workers often see people at their worst. **Caseloads** are often high. Sometimes the problems they deal with are overwhelming. **Burnout** is common in this line of work. Social workers can only help others if they help themselves. That's why self-care is especially important.

Healthy eating habits and regular exercise can help. So can the use of calming techniques like deep breathing and **meditation**. Establishing boundaries between their work and personal lives is especially important.

CHAPTER 3

Social Workers Know... The Tools of the Trade

Like other careers, social workers need special tools to do their jobs. Their toolboxes are not full of hammers and saws. Instead, they use special skills, therapies, and technologies to help their clients.

Social workers know how to connect with people. They can relate to all kinds of people. They work with people of all genders, income levels, and occupations. They work with all kinds of families of every nationality. The ability to honor diversity and **inclusivity** are necessary tools.

Social workers are also good listeners. They ask the right questions in interviews. This gets them the information they need to understand what is going on. They communicate with empathy and act with compassion.

Social workers are compassionate. They listen to their clients. They don't dismiss what they say.

Social workers typically work on cases involving multiple clients. It is not unusual for social workers to have very large caseloads. This makes recordkeeping an important tool. They take careful notes about everything they do. Assessments, treatment plans, and referrals are all recorded in a client's case file.

Technology helps social workers stay organized. They use special software to keep track of appointments and track client progress. They often rely on video conferencing tools to provide therapy sessions.

THE MOTHER OF SOCIAL WORK

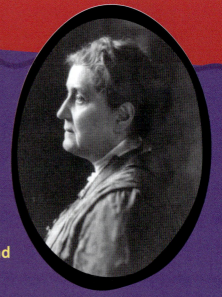

Jane Addams is known as the person who started social work. She cofounded Hull House in Chicago in 1889. This was a settlement house where poor people and immigrants could live. It provided social services and education.

Addams was also famous for speaking out as an advocate. She pushed for safer labor laws and better living conditions for the poor. In 1931, she became the first U.S. woman to be awarded the Nobel Peace Prize.

Group therapy offers lots of benefits, such as learning from diverse perspectives and improving communication skills.

In order to help clients, social workers may use techniques and therapies that are similar to those used by a psychologist. They may use behavior therapy to help a client modify unhealthy behaviors. They may use play therapy with children to help them work through **trauma**. Family therapy is used to help families communicate and strengthen relationships. Group therapy brings people with similar problems together to learn from others.

CHAPTER 4

Social Workers Know... How to Work Safely

Safety is a major concern for social workers. They often work with people experiencing high-stress situations. Clients may act out of anger, fear, or confusion. They may be in danger of harming themselves or others. Clients may also live in unsafe housing or neighborhoods.

The best way to stay safe is to be prepared. Social workers are careful to identify high-risk situations. They have been trained to follow certain rules. For instance, they check in with coworkers before and after home visits.

They make sure that their cell phone is fully charged and emergency contact information is readily available. They may also carry a panic button or alarm. This way, others can be alerted if help is needed. In high-risk situations, it is sometimes necessary to involve the police.

Social workers often turn to coworkers for help and guidance.

Maintaining a calm environment builds trust.

In all situations, social workers stay aware of their surroundings. They identify escape routes so they can leave quickly if problems arise.

Clear communication sets a professional tone. Social workers set boundaries so clients understand expectations. It is important to stay calm even when clients are not. Using a neutral tone of voice can help keep tense situations under control.

Social workers learn strategies to manage tense situations. Active listening, conflict resolution, and appropriate body language are helpful tools to keep everyone safe. A social worker's goal is to build trust so that clients are comfortable with them.

A BRIGHTER FUTURE

Every year, more than 1.2 million students drop out of high school in the United States. That's one student every 26 seconds, or 7,000 students a day. Social workers know that these students face an unemployment rate that is 47 percent higher than graduates. They know that students who drop out are more likely to engage in high-risk behavior. They also know that these students make up nearly half of the prison population.

This is why school social workers work extra hard to prevent students from dropping out. They try to identify students at risk as early as possible. They take steps to engage them in positive ways. They celebrate each graduation.

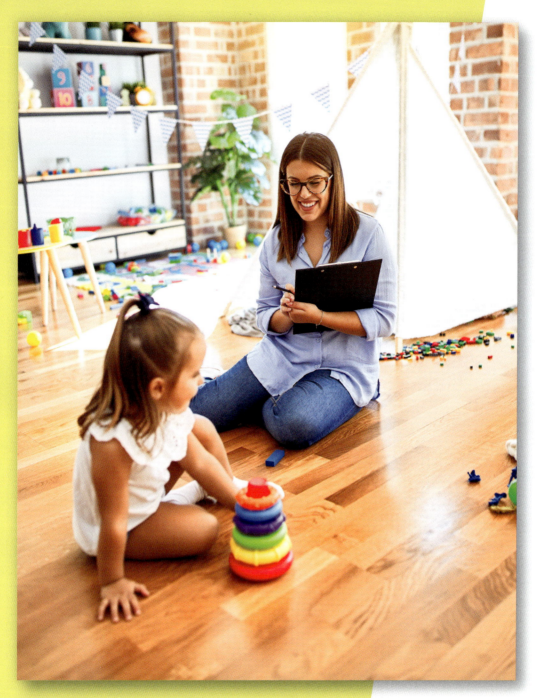

Social workers often take notes even while speaking or playing with a client. Even small details can be important for finding solutions.

Social workers have lots of paperwork. Every meeting with every client has to be recorded.

It is important for social workers to keep records every time they meet with a client. They must document any incidents or safety concerns. This protects both the client and the social worker. Good safety practices reduce risks and improve outcomes for their clients.

CHAPTER 5

Social Workers Know... How to Find the Job They Want

Social workers must earn a college degree. Some opportunities require a **bachelor's degree**. Even more opportunities are available with a **master's degree**. This adds another 2 years or so of schooling. Social workers must also complete a licensing process. This includes on-the-job practice and a test.

Once licensed, social workers have a variety of career paths to choose from. Some of these paths involve working with children or elderly people. Some involve working in hospitals or child protection agencies. Social workers choose the group of people they most want to serve. They also make important choices about the types of problems they want to solve.

It's important to stay focused in school to reach your goals. Social workers have to study hard to become licensed.

Clinical social workers help clients work through problems with therapy and counseling. They may work with individuals or groups. Like psychologists, they help diagnose and treat mental health conditions.

Child welfare social workers work with children. They work to make sure children have safe and loving places to grow up. They work to improve family situations. In some cases, they help children settle into foster care or adoption.

Other types of social workers include those who work with students in school settings. **Geriatric** social workers work with the elderly in hospitals and nursing homes.

HELP WANTED

There is no doubt about the fact that social workers help communities. Their usefulness explains why this career is one of the fastest-growing careers in the United States. The U.S. Department of Labor expects to see an average of 67,300 job openings for social workers every year for the next decade. Demand will be highest for child, family, and school social workers.

Health care social workers help patients navigate their conditions. They help them plan for the future.

Mental health and substance use social workers assess and treat clients to improve their mental and emotional health. They also help those who struggle with alcohol and other substance dependence.

People with serious health problems often find help from health care social workers. These social workers help patients get the care they need to cope with life-threatening diseases. One of their jobs is to connect patients with community resources for support.

Activity

Stop, Think, and Write

Can you imagine a world without social workers? How do they make the places we live, work, and play better?

Get a separate sheet of paper. On one side, answer this question:

- *How do social workers make the world a better place?*

On the other side of the paper:

- *Draw a picture of you helping a family in need.*

Things to Do If You Want to Be a Social Worker

Interested in helping people in crisis in your community? Then social work may be the career for you! Here are some things you can do to start preparing for this fulfilling career:

NOW

- Ask an adult to help you volunteer at a food bank or soup kitchen.
- Get involved in your school's student-to-student problem-solving or peer mediation group.
- Talk to your school counselor or social worker about what their job is like.
- Learn to be a good listener.

LATER

- Earn a bachelor's degree in social work, psychology, sociology, or behavioral science.
- Earn a master's degree in clinical social work.
- Get practical on-the-job experience.
- Pass the Association of Social Work Boards (ASWB) exam to earn certification.
- Obtain a state social work license.

Learn More

Books

Bussolari, Cori. *Empathy Is Your Superpower.* Emeryville, CA: Rockridge Press, 2021.

Learmonth, Amanda. *I Like Helping People … What Jobs Are There?* Tulsa, OK: Kane Miller, 2021.

Wilson, Timisha K. *A Kids Book About Social Workers.* Portland, OR: A Kids Co., 2025.

On the Web

With an adult, learn more online with these suggested searches.

Britannica Kids — Social Worker

Kiddle — Social Work Facts for Kids

National Association of Social Workers — Why Choose the Social Work Profession

Glossary

advocacy (AD-vuh-kuh-see) act of publicly supporting or recommending a particular cause or policy

assess (uh-SES) judge or evaluate the importance of something

bachelor's degree (BACH-luhrz dih-GREE) 4-year college degree

burnout (BUHRN-owt) physical and emotional exhaustion caused by prolonged stress

caseloads (KAYS-lohdz) number of cases assigned to one social worker

collaborate (kuh-LAA-buh-rayt) work together for a common purpose

first responders (FUHRST rih-SPAHN-duhrz) people whose job it is to respond to emergency situations

geriatric (jair-ee-AA-trik) related to the branch of medicine that serves elderly people

immigrants (IH-muh-gruhnts) people who relocate from one country to another

inclusivity (in-kloo-SIH-vuh-tee) process of welcoming everyone

intervene (in-tuhr-VEEN) get involved in a situation in order to change it

master's degree (MAA-stuhrz dih-GREE) graduate degree in a chosen academic subject

meditation (meh-duh-TAY-shuhn) act of thinking deeply and quietly in order to relax

trauma (TRAH-muh) an emotional shock that can affect a person for a long time

Index

activities, 30
Addams, Jane, 18
advocacy, 14–15, 18
assessments, 10, 12, 18

boundaries, 15, 22
burnout, 15

caseloads, 15, 18
child welfare workers, 28
clinical social workers, 28
community resources, 6, 8, 12–15, 29
compassion, 4–5, 9, 16–17
crisis management, 5, 15, 20, 22–23

diversity values, 16
documentation, 18, 24–25

education, 4, 23, 26–27, 30
empathy, 4–5, 9, 16

family therapy, 19
food resources, 6, 14–15, 30

geriatric welfare workers, 28
group therapy, 19

health care social work, 12–13, 29
human behavior and needs, 10, 15–16, 20, 22

immigrants, 6, 8, 18
inclusivity values, 16
interventions, 6, 8, 12

job market, 26, 28

mental health social workers, 28–29

privacy issues, 10
problem-solving, 4–6, 8–10, 12, 19, 26, 28–30

recordkeeping, 18, 24–25

safety, 20–25
school social workers, 8, 23, 28, 30
social workers
    job descriptions, 4, 6–26, 28–29
    stress and self-care, 15
    traits and skills, 4–5, 9, 15, 30
students, 8, 23
study and training, 4, 26–27, 30
substance abuse social workers, 29

therapies, 16, 18–19, 28
tools, 9, 15–19